LET'S GET ZAPPING...

SO WHAT SHOULD YOU BE ZAPPING IN THE ANNUAL?

Wherever you see the **interactive icon** you'll be able to unlock a fun experience to enjoy on your device. There are 15 scattered throughout the book to discover.

See if you can find them all.

READY.

Open Zappar on your device and find the Zapcode in the menu.

AIM.

Tap the Zapcode icon in the menu and scan the code on the page to download the content to your device.

ZAP.

Then point your device at the page and watch it come to life.

A FEW HELPFUL TIPS...

To get the best possible experience here are a few hints and tips:

- Connect to wifi if you can and the experiences will download even quicker than on 3G.

- Try and keep the pages as flat as you can for the best effect. Rest the book on a table or on the floor.

- Try and keep the full page in view from your phone after scanning the code. Don't get too close or far away if you can help it.

- Try and keep the pages clean and free from tears, pen and other marks as this may affect the experience.

- It's best to view the pages in good lighting conditions if you can.

If you're still having problems then do contact us at **support@zappar.com** and we'll do our best to help you.

CONTENTS

6 - WELCOME AND MEET THE CHARACTERS

8 - SONIC'S PROFILE

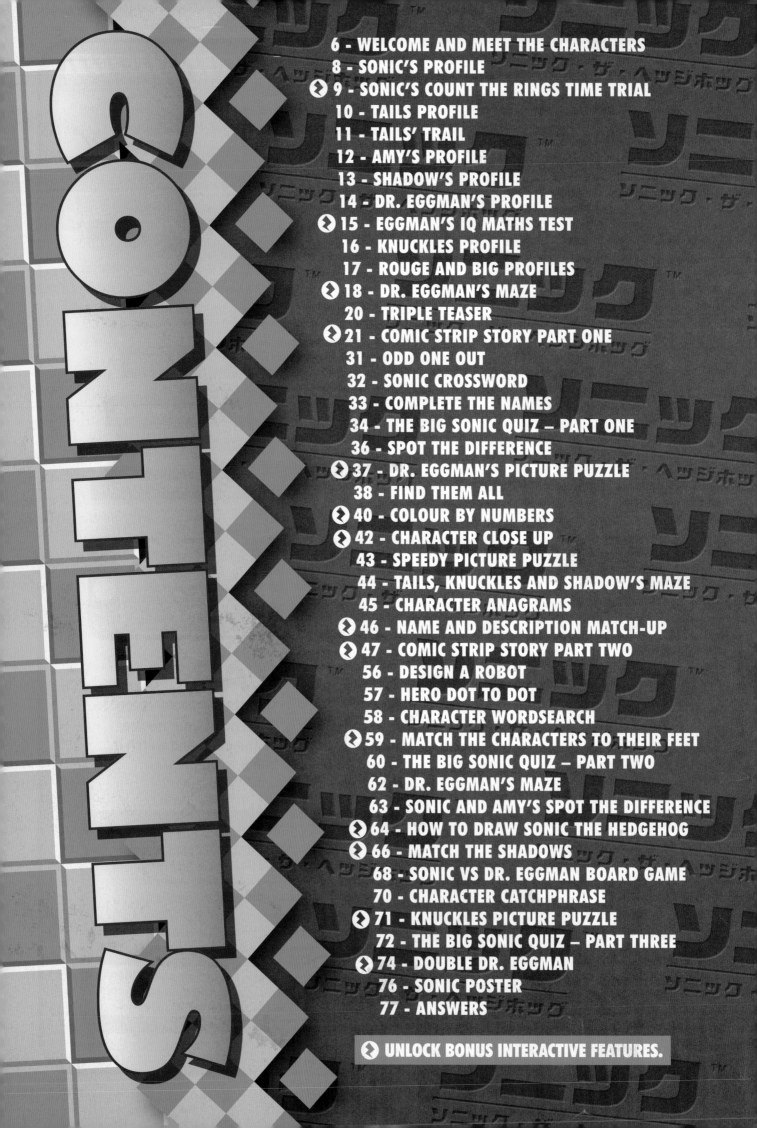 9 - SONIC'S COUNT THE RINGS TIME TRIAL

10 - TAILS PROFILE

11 - TAILS' TRAIL

12 - AMY'S PROFILE

13 - SHADOW'S PROFILE

14 - DR. EGGMAN'S PROFILE

15 - EGGMAN'S IQ MATHS TEST

16 - KNUCKLES PROFILE

17 - ROUGE AND BIG PROFILES

18 - DR. EGGMAN'S MAZE

20 - TRIPLE TEASER

21 - COMIC STRIP STORY PART ONE

31 - ODD ONE OUT

32 - SONIC CROSSWORD

33 - COMPLETE THE NAMES

34 - THE BIG SONIC QUIZ – PART ONE

36 - SPOT THE DIFFERENCE

37 - DR. EGGMAN'S PICTURE PUZZLE

38 - FIND THEM ALL

40 - COLOUR BY NUMBERS

42 - CHARACTER CLOSE UP

43 - SPEEDY PICTURE PUZZLE

44 - TAILS, KNUCKLES AND SHADOW'S MAZE

45 - CHARACTER ANAGRAMS

46 - NAME AND DESCRIPTION MATCH-UP

47 - COMIC STRIP STORY PART TWO

56 - DESIGN A ROBOT

57 - HERO DOT TO DOT

58 - CHARACTER WORDSEARCH

59 - MATCH THE CHARACTERS TO THEIR FEET

60 - THE BIG SONIC QUIZ – PART TWO

62 - DR. EGGMAN'S MAZE

63 - SONIC AND AMY'S SPOT THE DIFFERENCE

64 - HOW TO DRAW SONIC THE HEDGEHOG

66 - MATCH THE SHADOWS

68 - SONIC VS DR. EGGMAN BOARD GAME

70 - CHARACTER CATCHPHRASE

71 - KNUCKLES PICTURE PUZZLE

72 - THE BIG SONIC QUIZ – PART THREE

74 - DOUBLE DR. EGGMAN

76 - SONIC POSTER

77 - ANSWERS

UNLOCK BONUS INTERACTIVE FEATURES.

SUPER INTERACTIVE ANNUAL 2014

SONIC™
THE HEDGEHOG

Pedigree

Published 2013. Pedigree Books Limited, Beech Hill House, Walnut Gardens, Exeter, Devon EX4 4DH.
www.pedigreebooks.com – books@pedigreegroup.co.uk

WELCOME!

Welcome to the Sonic the Hedgehog 2014 Super Interactive Annual, the perfect book for all true Sonic fans! With over 70 pages of stories, interesting facts and mind bending activities, this Annual is so awesome that you'll never want to put it down... Apart from when you're checking out the interactive content!

In a moment, we'll introduce you to the characters, but first here's a bit more information about what else you'll find in this Annual...

CHARACTER PROFILES

Everything you need to know about Sonic, his friends and his rivals.

ACTIVITIES AND PUZZLES

From word searches to spot the difference puzzles, colour by numbers to dot to dot drawings, this Super Interactive Annual has plenty going on to keep you occupied.

COMIC STRIP STORIES

Read up on Sonic's latest adventures in some awesomely illustrated comic strip stories and follow our blue hero and his friends as they continue to save the world!

As you will have seen there is even more to this book than what simply appears on the pages, thanks to the extra interactive sections that allow you to access cool bonus content on a mobile phone or tablet device.

Quite simply, there's so much going on in this book that you'll need to be as speedy and sharp as Sonic to get through everything. So, what are you waiting for? Let's get started!

MEET THE CHARACTERS

Over the next few pages you will find out much more about each character, but to start with, here's a list of who is featured in this book...

SONIC

DR. EGGMAN

TAILS

ROUGE

AMY

BIG

SHADOW

KNUCKLES

Profile

Interesting Info...

Sonic runs faster than the speed of light and according to the Guinness Book of Records, he is officially the fastest video game character of all time!

SONIC

The speediest, quickest, fastest, most rapid character in the world. Sonic is one hyped up, enthusiastic, life-loving hedgehog, who uses his bravery, pace and confidence to help save the world.

Living in a world filled with fun, excitement and adventure, Sonic is a cool character who is always good to his friends and looks awesome whether he's standing still (never for long) or buzzing around in a blue blaze of energy!

Sonic is good friends with Tails and Amy and the trio work together to defeat our blue hero's greatest rival, the evil Dr. Eggman. Although he may occasionally have a short fuse, Sonic has a big heart and is always happy to help out his friends and anybody who is in trouble.

Name:........Sonic the Hedgehog
Age:............15
Height:......100cm
Weight:......35kg

Did You Know?
Sonic's nemesis, Dr. Eggman, has an IQ of 300!

SONIC'S COUNT THE RINGS TIME TRIAL

By now you know just how speedy Sonic the Hedgehog is, but this activity gives you the chance to prove your pace and show just how rapid you can be. This page is covered in golden rings and all you need to do is to count them all, as quickly as possible! Grab a watch or a clock, or use the timer on your phone or tablet and time how long it takes to count every single golden ring!

Once you think you've counted all the rings, stop the clock and check page 77 to see if you've managed to spot every single one!

Answer:

Clue...
There are over 50 rings on this page!

Profile

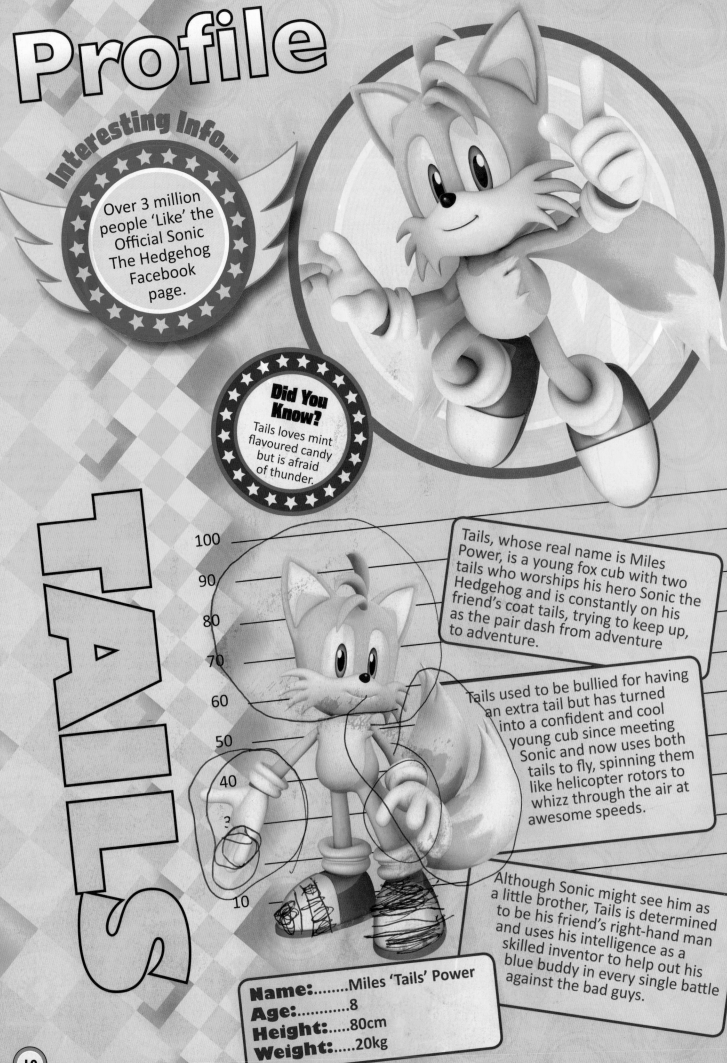

Did You Know?
Tails loves mint flavoured candy but is afraid of thunder.

TAILS

100
90
80
70
60
50
40
3?
10

Tails, whose real name is Miles Power, is a young fox cub with two tails who worships his hero Sonic the Hedgehog and is constantly on his friend's coat tails, trying to keep up, as the pair dash from adventure to adventure.

Tails used to be bullied for having an extra tail but has turned into a confident and cool young cub since meeting Sonic and now uses both tails to fly, spinning them like helicopter rotors to whizz through the air at awesome speeds.

Although Sonic might see him as a little brother, Tails is determined to be his friend's right-hand man and uses his intelligence as a skilled inventor to help out his blue buddy in every single battle against the bad guys.

Name:........Miles 'Tails' Power
Age:............8
Height:.....80cm
Weight:.....20kg

Tails usually manages to keep up with his great friend Sonic, well most of the time anyway! But, he has fallen a little behind his best bud. Can you complete this tricky trail to help him catch up with Sonic? One of the three winding jungle trails follows the journey taken by Sonic, with the other two leading to precious emeralds. You can't really go wrong in this challenge but if you end up at one of the emeralds, go back to the beginning and try to find the trail that reunites Tails with his blue companion...

You can find the correct trail on page 77.

TAILS' TRAIL

11

Profile

Amy Rose loves soft-serve ice cream and she hates being bored.

Name:........Amy Rose
Age:............12
Height:.....90cm
Weight:.....Secret!

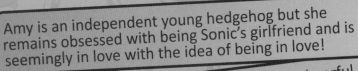

Amy is an independent young hedgehog but she remains obsessed with being Sonic's girlfriend and is seemingly in love with the idea of being in love!

Although Amy is one of the most cheerful characters, her friends and rivals know that she isn't a pushover, especially when she's armed with her Piko Piko hammer and ready for battle.

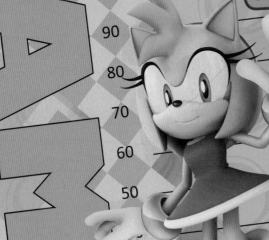

100

90

80

70

60

50

30

20

10

Design Amy a New Outfit

One of the best dressed characters around, Amy looks rocking in red, wearing a cool dress and matching shoes, but do you think you can make her look any cooler? Use whatever colours you like to fill in this outline of Amy and design a new outfit that will impress Sonic...

Did You Know?
Sonic loves DJ-ing

Profile

Did You Know?
Sonic's favourite food is Chilli dogs!

SHADOW

Name:........Shadow the Hedgehog
Age:............ Unknown
Height:.....100cm
Weight:.....35kg

He may look like Sonic in many ways and be just as quick as his fellow hedgehog, but Shadow is a very different character who is prepared to do whatever it takes to save the world.

Thanks to his special jet powered boots, Shadow shares Sonic's agility and speed but he remains a mysterious character. The 'Ultimate Life Form' created by Dr. Eggman's grandfather - the genius scientist Professor Gerald - Shadow has a special power called 'Chaos Control' which allows him to use the Chaos Emerald to warp time and space.

Shadow Dot to Dot

Control the chaos and bring Shadow out of the dark by completing this tricky dot to dot to reveal the spitting image of Sonic.

Profile

DR. EGGMAN

Interesting Info...

Sonic's birthday is June 23rd and he was born on Christmas Island.

A brilliant but mad scientist, Dr. Eggman prefers to use his intelligence for evil as he attempts to take over the world and turn it into Eggman Land. With an ego almost as big as his IQ, which is over 300, he prides himself on being an evil genius.

Thankfully, the determined doctor's plans are usually foiled by Sonic, but he remains obsessed with getting the better of the blue hero, even if he does secretly admire the speedy hedgehog.

Name:........Dr. Eggman
Age:............Unknown
Height:......185cm
Weight:......128kg

Did You Know?

Even though Sonic can't swim, he is able to run across the surface of water.

EGGMAN'S IQ MATHS TEST

Evil Genius Dr. Eggman has an amazingly high IQ of 300. With this brain teasing activity you can test just how smart you are by completing all of these math sums. Each answer adds up to 300 but you need to fill each answer in every box to show how you've worked it out to get the points. There are five questions, can you complete them all?

For example... $10 + 40 = 50 \times 2 = 100 \times 3 = 300$

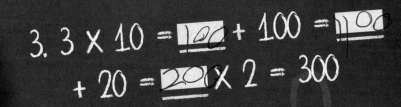

1. $25 \times 4 = \boxed{500} + 50 = \boxed{600} + 50 = \boxed{200} + 100 = 300$

2. $500 - 300 = \boxed{100} + 10 = \boxed{100} + 50 = \boxed{10} + 50 = \boxed{110} - 10 = 300$

3. $3 \times 10 = \boxed{100} + 100 = \boxed{100} + 20 = \boxed{200} \times 2 = 300$

4. $10 \times 10 = \boxed{110} + 100 = \boxed{110} + 200 = \boxed{900} - 100 = 300$

5. $100 + 50 = \boxed{100} - 100 = \boxed{200} + 200 = \boxed{200} + 20 = \boxed{111} + 10 = \boxed{208} + 20 = 300$

See page 77 for the answers.

Profile

Knuckles loves fruit, especially grapes.

KNUCKLES

100
90
80
70
60

20

Heroic, brave and one of Sonic's main rivals, Knuckles the Echidna lives on an island in the sky called Angel Island where he guards a giant Master Emerald that only he can control.

Knuckles usually disagrees with Sonic, with the speedy hedgehog keen to run around at 100 miles per hour and the slower, steadier Echidna often taking life too seriously.

Name:......Knuckles the Echidna
Age:..........16
Height:...110cm
Weight:...40kg

Did You Know?
Sonic always tries to avoid water as he is unable to swim, just like Tails.

Knuckles Spot the Difference

Scan these two pictures of Sonic and Knuckles. There are five differences between each picture. You're probably not used to seeing these two standing still so look with extra care to try and spot all five differences...

Colour in a star for each difference.

☆☆☆☆☆

ROUGE

Name:......Rouge the Bat
Age:..........18
Height:...105cm
Weight:...Unknown

A wild, sharply dressed bat, who is sleek enough to fly around at awesome speed, Rouge's specialist subject is treasure-hunting for jewels and she uses all of her charms to collect as many as possible.

Although Rouge is on Sonic's side, some of the time, she actually prefers to join forces with Shadow, as long as there's something in it for her of course!

Interesting Info...

Rouge likes to calls herself the 'World's Greatest Thief.'

Did You Know?

Knuckles the Echidna has super-strength spiked knuckles.

Name:......Big the Cat
Age:..........18
Height:...200cm
Weight:...280kg

Cool cat Big is a gentle giant who loves to chill out in the wild by fishing, eating, sleeping and chatting to his friend, Froggy the Frog.

This giant feline may be laid back most of the time, preferring to live the easy life, but if Big or his friends are in trouble he can certainly show his teeth. The peace-loving cat possesses awesome strength and can lift up all kinds of objects to launch at his enemies.

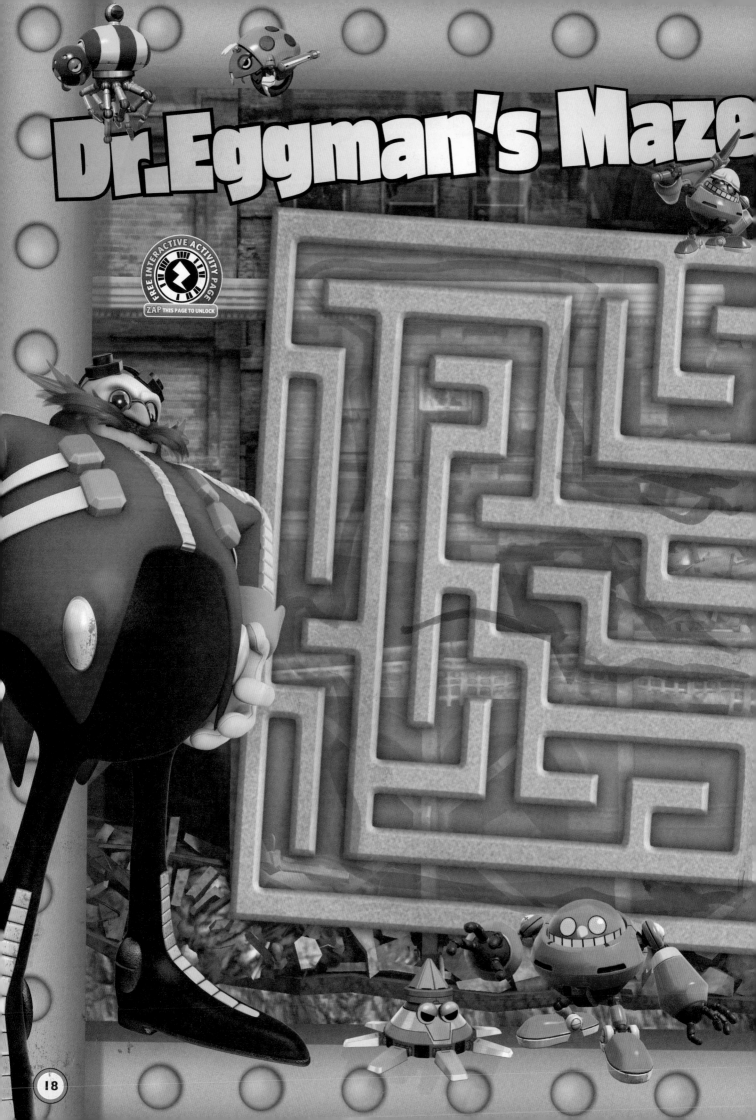

Dr. Eggman's Maze

FREE INTERACTIVE ACTIVITY PAGE

ZAP THIS PAGE TO UNLOCK

Sonic was sprinting around at his usual awesome speed until he reached this confusing metallic maze, which was built by Dr. Eggman. There are lots of dead ends but only one way out. Grab a pen or a pencil and try and find the right route to set Sonic free and back on his journey.

END

START

You can find the correct trail on page 77.

19

TRIPLE TEASER
Quick Quiz, Mini Wordsearch, Secret Word

This activity is divided into three different levels so you'll need to keep your wits about you to complete each task and eventually work out the final answer.

First up is a quick fire five-question quiz. Once you've worked out the answers write them down in the spaces provided. Then it's time to move on to the mini wordsearch. Hidden inside this grid of letters is a quick-fire, five question quiz.

Circle or highlight each word as you find it in the wordsearch. Once you've found them all, make a note of all the letters left in the grid that aren't part of any of the five words. Write these letters down in the space provided and then try to workout out which Sonic the Hedgehog related word or phrase they make up.

For example, if you are left with the letters C O I N and S they can be moved around to make the word SONIC.

Good luck, let's get cracking with the Quick-Fire Quiz...

1. He is known as the Ultimate Lifeform?

_____

2. Knuckles lives on _ _ _ _ _ Island?

_____

3. Sonic is blue, but what colour is Shadow?

_____

4. What is Sonic's best friend called?

_____

5. What is the second part of Amy's name?

_____

E	G	U	O	R	W
B	O	I	N	S	O
D	L	C	H	A	D
E	G	A	N	H	A
O	G	G	C	T	H
E	E	H	E	K	S
L	T	A	I	L	S

Remaining letters:

_____

Final Answer:

_____

WELCOME BACK TO THE PLANET **MOBIUS**--A WORLD UNIQUE AND BEYOND WHAT YOU KNOW FROM THE **SEGA** GAMES--WHERE **SONIC** AND THE HEROIC **FREEDOM FIGHTERS** WORK TO SAVE THE WORLD FROM THE FORCES OF **EVIL**!

LOST IN THE MOMENT

SONIC THE HEDGEHOG
HERO OF MOBIUS

HEDGEHOG. PRIORITY ONE.

NO... SAL...

HA HA HA HA HA HA HA!

MECHA SALLY
ROBOT SLAVE

DOCTOR EGGMAN
MAD GENIUS

BWAHAHAHA!

WRITER: IAN FLYNN • PENCILS AND COVER: BEN BATES
INKS: TERRY AUSTIN • COLORS: MATT HERMS • LETTERS: JOHN WORKMAN
EDITOR: PAUL KAMINSKI • EDITOR-IN-CHIEF: VICTOR GORELICK
PRESIDENT: MIKE PELLERITO
SPECIAL THANKS TO ANTHONY GACCIONE AND CINDY CHAU
AT SEGA LICENSING

GOOD GIRL.

THANK YOU, SIR. YOUR WORD IS LAW.

OH-HO-HO! SO IT IS! SNIVELY! PREPARE FOR A FULL ASSAULT!

⸗KZZT!⸗ BUT, SIR...! ⸗BZZZT!⸗

I DON'T CARE HOW DAMAGED WE ARE! I HAVE A DEATH EGG, IT'S GOT A CHAOS EMERALD, AND WE CAN DESTROY NEW MOBOTROPOLIS BEFORE SONIC HITS THE GROUND!

THAT'S JUST IT! ⸗KSSSK⸗ THE CHAOS EMERALD IS GONE!

...WHAT ?

I DON'T ⸗BZZZT!⸗ WHEN IT HAPPENED, BUT THE ROBOTICIZER BLEW ⸗KSSSK!⸗ AND WE'RE RUN-NING LOW ON POWER!

OF ALL THE BLASTED...AND JUST WHEN I THOUGHT I HAD THAT "CHAOS FACTOR" IN MY FAVOR! FULL RETREAT! LAUNCH PROJECTS "TITAN" AND "DEADLY CUDDLES" TO DELAY THEM! MECHA SALLY, COME WITH ME...

I NEED TO COME UP WITH A BETTER NAME FOR YOU.

YES, SIR.

THIS SCENE IS GRUESOME ENOUGH WITHOUT YOU HERE, TOO!
CURB YOUR INSOLENCE AND HELP ME DESTROY THIS MENACE!
HELP!
WHAT IS THAT THING?!
RUN!

INTERACTIVE COMIC!

IF YOU ENJOYED READING THAT COOL COMIC STRIP STORY, THERE'S ANOTHER ONE WAITING FOR YOU ON YOUR TABLET OR PHONE. JUST SCAN THE ICON TO ENJOY ANOTHER ADVENTURE...

ODD ONE OUT

Check out these images of Sonic, Tails, Dr. Eggman and Shadow. There are three pictures of each character and at first glance they all look identical. However, one of the three images is slightly different. Look hard to see which image is different and why...

SONIC CROSSWORD

In this teasing crossword, Sonic has set you another task to test your sharpness. Scan through all the clues and write the correct answers in the crossword grid. The answers go across and down so make sure you match up the right answer to the right number.

Across

1. The type of animal that both Shadow and Sonic are (8 letters)
2. Shadow has a special power called Chaos _ _ _ _ _ _ _ (7 letters)
3. Knuckles is an _ _ _ _ _ _ _ (7 letters)
4. Complete Rouge's name (6 letters)
5. An evil scientist with a huge IQ (7 letters)

Down

1. He looks just like Sonic but is black instead of blue (6 letters)
2. Sonic's most trusted companion (5 letters)
3. The fastest moving character in the world (5 letters)
4. Amy uses a Piko Piko what? (6 letters)
5. The full name of the female hedgehog who loves Sonic (7 letters)

Interesting Info...

When Shadow becomes Super Shadow, he is able to fly.

SONIC & ALL★STARS RACING TRANSFORMED

COMPLETE THE NAMES

Knuckles has been burrowing underground and set off an avalanche which has caused some of the letters in these words to drop below the soil and out of sight. But now with several letters missing they just don't make any sense. Try to use the letters you can see to work out what Knuckles has dislodged and then fill in the gaps to complete each character's name...

1. __ R __ G __ MA __
2. T __ __ S
3. __ H __ DW
4. K __ __ CK __ __ S
5. R __ __ G __ H __ B __ __
6. B __ __ T __ __ CT __
7. __ OI __
8. A __ __ RS __

THE BIG SONIC QUIZ PART ONE

1. Knuckles lives in an island in the sky...
   True or False?

2. Tails has a total of three tails...
   True or False?

3. Rouge is a big cat... **True or False?**

4. Sonic can run faster than the speed of sound... **True or False?**

5. Amy uses a Pinko Pinko hammer to defend herself... **True or False?**

6. Big the Cat's best friend is called Moggy...
   True or False?

7. Knuckles is a martial arts expert...
   True or False?

8. Tails is afraid of thunder...
   True or False?

9. Amy is in love with Shadow...
   True or False?

10. Cheese burgers are Sonic's favourite food...
    True or False?

By now you know pretty much all there is to know about Sonic, the other good guys and the bad guys, but part one of The Big Sonic Quiz should test just how much you've remembered.

Over the next two pages there are 20 questions to test even the biggest Sonic the Hedgehog fan. You need to decide whether the statement in each question is true or false. Dr. Eggman has interfered with this quiz so watch out for a few trick questions!

Part Two of The Big Sonic Quiz can be found on page 60

11. Dr. Eggman wears a red jacket...
True or False?

12. Amy is taller than Tails...
True or False?

13. Sonic wears blue shoes...
True or False?

14. Shadow was created by Dr. Eggman's grandfather...
True or False?

15. Knuckles can burrow like a mole...
True or False?

16. Sonic cannot swim...
True or False?

17. Rouge loves to treasure hunt for jewels...
True or False?

18. Big the Cat loves eating and sleeping...
True or False?

19. Tails full name is Tails Miles Power...
True or False?

20. Dr. Eggman is taller than Big the Cat...
True or False?

SPOT THE DIFFERENCE

Concentrate hard on these two pictures of Sonic, Tails, Amy and Knuckles. They may both look alike but there are actually five differences between picture one and picture two. Some might be obvious but others will be harder to spot. Good luck...

1

2

DR. EGGMAN'S PICTURE PUZZLE

Dr.EGGMAN

Dr. Eggman has come up with another tough task with this picture puzzle activity. He has used one of his most complex robots to jumble up these three pictures of three of the characters. It's not going to be easy to identify who's who, but all you can do is try your best...

FREE INTERACTIVE ACTIVITY PAGE
ZAP THIS PAGE TO UNLOCK

1. ANSWER

2. ANSWER

3. ANSWER

Interesting Info...

Both Sonic and Shadow can perform spin attacks by rolling themselves up into a ball.

FIND THEM ALL

Sonic and the other good guys are hiding from Dr. Eggman and the bad guys, but the bad guys are doing the same, lying in wait to try and surprise our heroes. Carefully scan your eyes across this picture of Green Hill and try and find them all.

Remember you're looking for...Sonic, Tails, Amy, Knuckles, Big the Cat and... Dr. Eggman, Shadow and Rouge the Bat.

★ Sonic,

★ Tails

★ Amy

★ Knuckles

★ Big the Cat

★ Dr. Eggman

★ Shadow

★ Rouge the Bat

COLOUR BY NUMBERS

Hopefully you managed to find all of the characters hidden in Green Hill in the previous activity. This time you just need to focus on the good guys. Help Sonic to colour in this sketched image of Tails, Amy and Knuckles. Use the key below as your guide as each number is matched to a different colour to indicate how each blank space needs to be coloured in.

5

3

7

2

6

1

4

8

CHARACTER CLOSE UP

Check out these eight extreme close-ups of our characters and try to work out who is featured. The zoomed in pictures show just a small part of each character's body, face or clothing. You better keep your eyes peeled if you're going to work out all eight...

1.

2.

3.

4.

5.

6.

7.

8.

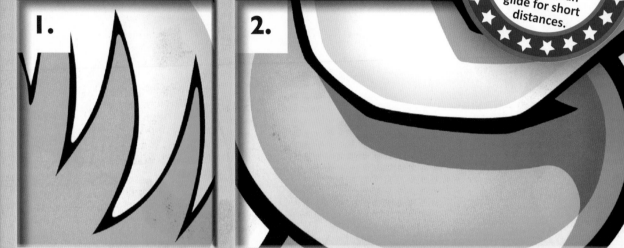

SPEEDY PICTURE PUZZLE

Sonic has run at such an amazing pace past each of these three characters that everything has become a bit of a blur. It's time for you to slow things down, take a breath and try and work out who's who...

Interesting Info...

Tails is able to push himself through the air to catch-up with Sonic, but usually tires quickly.

TAILS, KNUCKLES AND SHADOWS' MAZE

Sonic, Tails and Knuckles have been helping Shadow
look for his precious Chaos Emerald. The sneaky Dr. Eggman has
hidden it in the middle of a mind-bending maze. Sonic has been buzzing
around at a pace faster than the speed of sound as he triesto track down the Emerald but the
blue hero has been separated from his three friends. See where Tails, Knuckles and Shadow have
ended up and try to follow the maze to help them get their hands on the Chaos Emerald.
Be careful to make sure you avoid the dead ends!

Did You Know? Unlike Sonic, Tails is able to swim.

CHARACTER ANAGRAMS

Dr. Eggman has been up to his old tricks again and jumbled up the characters' names to form different words that all sound like the names of his robot-like inventions. Check out each word and try to work out the correct name...

1. COINS

2. GROUE

3. STAIL

4. WASHDO

5. GBI

6. AYM

7. SLUCKKEN

Interesting Info...

Knuckles uses the spikes on his knuckles to climb walls.

NAME AND DESCRIPTION MATCH-UP

You've learned a bit about Sonic and the other characters already, but how much can you remember? Check out these two lists, the first includes each of the character's names and the second contains a sentence that describes them. Draw a line to match the correct name to the correct description...

Interesting Info...

Tails loves tinkering with machines, especially those that can fly.

Big

Rouge

Dr. Eggman

Knuckles

Sonic

Tails

Amy

Shadow

This character has a special power called 'Chaos Control'.

This character can burrow like a mole.

His best friend is called Froggy.

This hedgehog wears pink and uses a Piko Piko hammer.

A loyal hedgehog who keeps his promises and never lets anybody down.

This fox cub is Sonic's most trusted companion.

A bat that loves hunting for jewels.

A mad scientist and an evil genius.

FREE INTERACTIVE ACTIVITY PAGE
ZAP THIS PAGE TO UNLOCK

SONIC
THE HEDGEHOG
:PRIMARY TARGET

PART TWO....

WE'VE LOST CONTACT WITH TITAN METAL SONIC! THE TORNADO AND ...IS THAT THE PRINCESS? IT STILL WORKED?!

PUT THE ENGINES ON RESERVE POWER! PUT EVERYTHING ELSE INTO THE EGG ANNIHILATOR BEAM AND FIRE ON NEW MOBOTROPOLIS!

BUT...

...WE'RE HEAVILY DAMAGED AND ALREADY RUNNING LOW ON...

MECHA SALLY?

DO AS THE MASTER COMMANDS!

EEP!

"GOOD GIRL. I STILL NEED A BETTER NAME FOR YOU, THOUGH..."

AFTER ALL THAT... WHAT ELSE DOES IT HAVE?!

BRRRRRRR

SHABLAM!

SERVE YOUR NEW MASTER, CRYSTAL GOLEM!

SKA-KOOM

GEOFFREY ST. JOHN
TRAITOR & IXIS
APPRENTICE

RAH-RAH! HOORAY! TO THE KING!

RAH! RAH! HOORAY! TO THE KING

WHY...WHY HASN'T NICOLE FIXED THIS YET...?

RAH-RAH! HOORAY! TO THE KING!

...REAL GRASS? NOT NANITES?

THERE YOU ARE, MR. SONIC! PLEASE, FOLLOW ME!

MAIS QU'EST-CE QUE--?!

IT'S MAGIC, COMMANDER. I CAN ONLY BEGIN TO GUESS.

RAH! RAH! HOORAY! TO THE KING!

RAH! RAH! HOORAY!

TO THE KING!

SHE'S STABLE, AT LEAST. YOU... HELP ME BRING HER TO THE HOSPITAL.

OKAY.

RAH! RAH! HOORAY! TO THE KING!

VANILLA! WHAT HAPPENED?

IT WAS DREADFUL!

FIRST THE GIANT ROBOT, AND THEN ALL THE LIGHTS AND EXPLOSIONS, THEN POOR MRS. D'COOLETTE...

...FELL, AND NOW THAT... THAT AWFUL WIZARD...!

RAH! RAH! HOORAY! TO THE KING!

SONIC...THE CHEERING...

IT'S NOT FOR US.

RAH! RAH! HOO-RAY! TO THE KING! NAUGUS! NAUGUS! NAUGUS!

RAH! RAH! HOORAY! TO THE KING!

HE STOPPED THE GIANT METAL SONIC!

HE SAVED US FROM THE DEATH EGG!

HE CAN PROTECT US FROM NICOLE AND DOCTOR EGGMAN!

WE WANT OUR NEW KING!

INTERACTIVE COMIC!

THAT WAS ANOTHER GREAT ADVENTURE INVOLVING SONIC THE HEDGEHOG AND HIS FRIENDS AND RIVALS. GET INTERACTIVE NOW TO READ MORE ABOUT THE BLUE HERO'S ADVENTURES IN THIS INTERACTIVE COMIC STRIP...

FREE INTERACTIVE ACTIVITY PAGE

ZAP THIS PAGE TO UNLOCK

DESIGN A ROBOT

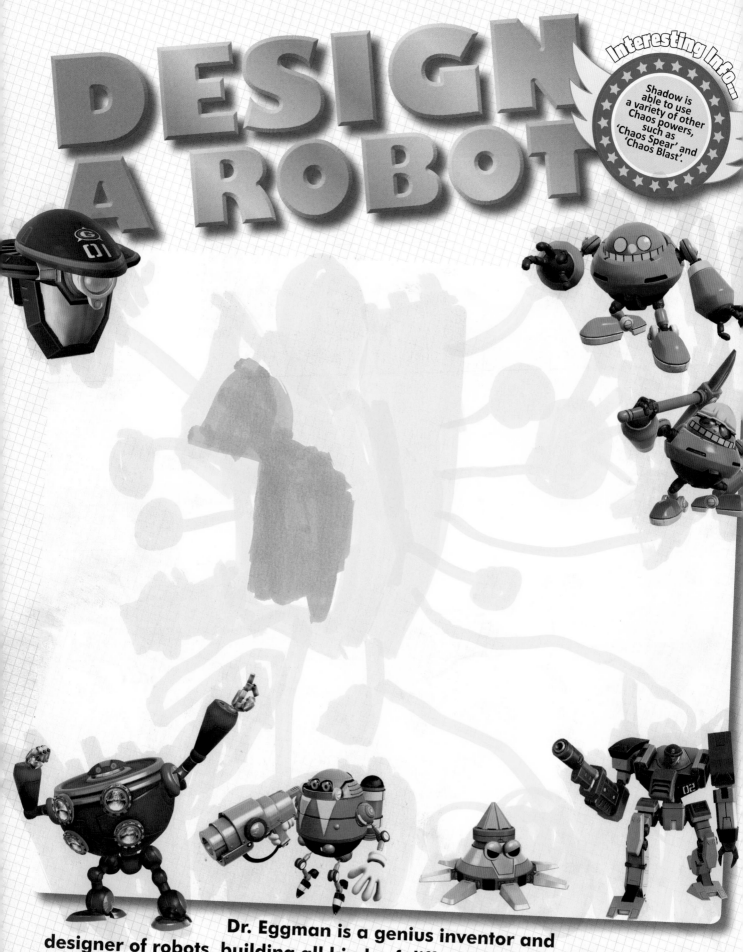

Dr. Eggman is a genius inventor and designer of robots, building all kinds of different mechanical contraptions as he tries to defeat Sonic and the other heroes, but have you got what it takes to create a machine to rival the mad scientist? Use this page to dream up the ultimate robot, thinking about what it would look like, what special powers it might have and how it might move around.

HERO DOT TO DOT

HIDDEN UNDER ALL OF THESE DOTS ARE TWO OF OUR HEROES, SIMPLY DRAW A LINE TO JOIN UP EACH OF THE DOTS AND REVEAL THEIR IDENTITIES. ONCE YOU'VE FINISHED, WHY NOT COLOUR THEM IN AS WELL?

CHARACTER WORDSEARCH

Scan through this grid of letters to find each of the characters, as well as a list of words associated with them. The words could be written forwards, backwards, horizontally, vertically and diagonally so keep your eyes peeled to find them all...

SONIC

ROUGE

RINGS

KNUCKLES

ECHIDNA

BIG

TAILS

HEDGEHOG

SHADOW

DR EGGMAN

FAST

FOX CUB

AMY

EMERALD

CHAOS

S	F	H	S	E	L	K	C	U	N	K	P	I
S	C	O	J	S	F	D	L	T	X	S	T	E	F
B	L	N	D	W	O	Z	A	F	S	T	A	B
I	I	B	I	R	L	B	S	R	W	S	Q	A
G	O	P	Y	C	E	L	S	Y	T	D	S	X
T	Y	M	O	V	W	P	W	U	S	T	O	W
T	A	K	L	P	I	Y	T	T	E	D	S	E
H	A	M	B	U	C	X	O	F	T	Z	G	E
U	O	I	B	N	M	J	R	T	S	U	N	L
Y	R	C	L	I	S	D	F	G	O	J	K	S
P	T	E	N	S	I	Y	T	R	F	V	M	W
E	P	B	D	S	D	L	L	E	M	C	I	O
G	O	H	E	G	D	E	H	D	C	H	R	D
H	B	N	M	H	G	V	L	T	Y	A	R	A
R	D	L	C	S	K	A	E	R	B	O	O	H
I	T	I	N	K	R	P	O	P	S	S	R	S
N	G	N	E	E	L	O	D	W	U	E	F	X
G	G	M	M	S	Y	L	B	N	S	T	I	P
S	E	E	H	S	G	N	I	R	A	E	T	P
S	J	F	N	E	N	A	M	G	G	E	R	D
E	C	H	I	D	N	A	S	P	J	U	S	X

Most of our characters are famed for the speed at which they can move across the ground, meaning that their feet are a really important part of how they generate such break-neck speeds. Check out the eight pictures below and see if you can work out which feet belong to who.

It should be a walk in the park!

MATCH THE CHARACTERS TO THEIR FEET

5 Rouge

8 Amy

3 Shadow

4 Dr. Eggman

7 Sonic

1 Big

2 Knuckles

6 Tails

THE BIG SONIC QUIZ PART TWO

In the second part of The Big Sonic Quiz the questions are getting slightly more difficult to answer. The next two pages feature another 20 questions that will test your Sonic the Hedgehog knowledge to the max! Once again, the crazy Scientist, Dr. Eggman has added even more confusing questions so be on your guard to make sure he doesn't defeat you. **Think what Sonic would do and try your very best...**

1. Tails used to be bullied before he met Sonic...
   True or False??

2. Big the Cat hates fishing...
   True or False?

3. Shadow has been described as the Ultimate Life Form...
   True or False?

4. Knuckles is unable to smash rocks with his fists...
   True or False?

5. Amy wears a purple and green dress ...
   True or False?

6. Froggy the Frog is best friends with Shadow...
   True or False?

7. Dr Eggman has an IQ of 300...
   True or False?

8. Sonic is 100cm tall...

True or False?

9. Tails is a talented inventor of machines...

True or False?

10. Knuckles is a hedgehog...

True or False?

11. Shadow wears black gloves...

True or False?

12. Big has been described as a gentle giant...

True or False?

13. Rouge cannot fly...

True or False?

14. Big is older than Knuckles...

True or False?

15. Shadow is an echidna...

True or False?

16. Amy is known as being really grumpy...

True or False?

17. Tails is younger than Sonic...

True or False?

18. Knuckles can glide and scale walls...

True or False?

19. Rouge hates jewels and other treasure...

True or False?

20. Dr. Eggman has black boots...

True or False?

DR. EGGMAN'S MAZE

Dr. Eggman has got himself in all kinds of tangles and twists as he tries to catch up with the ever speedy Sonic. Right now he's stuck in the middle of a maze in Green Hill that's filled with dead ends. There's only one way out... can you find it?

START

END

SONIC AND AMY'S SPOT THE DIFFERENCE

Check out these two pictures of Amy chasing the love of her life Sonic. Although Sonic is smiling he seems pretty keen to get away from young Amy Rose! Look closely at both picture one and picture two because there are five differences between them. Can you spot them all?

Colour in a star for each difference.

(stars)

HOW TO DRAW SONIC THE HEDGEHOG

Learn how to draw the perfect picture of Sonic the Hedgehog and bring our blue hero to life by following this simple step by step guide.

Use lines and circles to create Sonic's head, body shape and stance.

Using light pencil lines, carefully fill out Sonic's head and body shape.

Now it's time to add more detail by sketching in Sonic's clothes and facial features.

Finish your drawing by adding sharper pencil lines and accurately shading in the right colours.

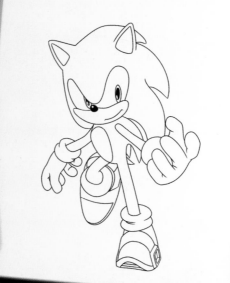

MATCH THE SHADOWS

1 shadow   **2** Dr.eggman   **3** sonic   **4** Knuckles

Shadow the Hedgehog is just like Sonic although he does have a slightly darker side. In this activity all of the characters have faced black out and been turned into silhouettes.

Can you work out who's who by simply looking at each Shadow?

See page 77 for the answers.

7

5

6

8

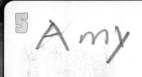

5 Amy

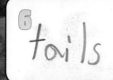

6 tails

7 Big

8 Rouge

SONIC Vs DR. EGGMAN BOARD GAME

Sonic is usually way fast enough to outrun Dr. Eggman and he is an expert at foiling the mad scientist's most destructive plans, but will that be the case in the Sonic versus Dr. Eggman Board Game?

Let's find out...

ANSWER THE QUESTIONS TO GET AROUND THE BOARD!

In this two player board game, one of the players has to be Sonic and the other has to be Dr. Eggman. You will need a dice and two counters to play this game.

Place your counters on the starting square. Take turns to roll the dice. Highest number goes first.

Sonic or Dr. Eggman squares: If you land on one of these and the face matches the character you have chosen, to move forward you can roll the dice again, but if it doesn't match the square then you miss a turn.

If you land on a square with golden rings, move forward one, two or three squares depending on the number of rings.

First one across the finishing ring wins the game!

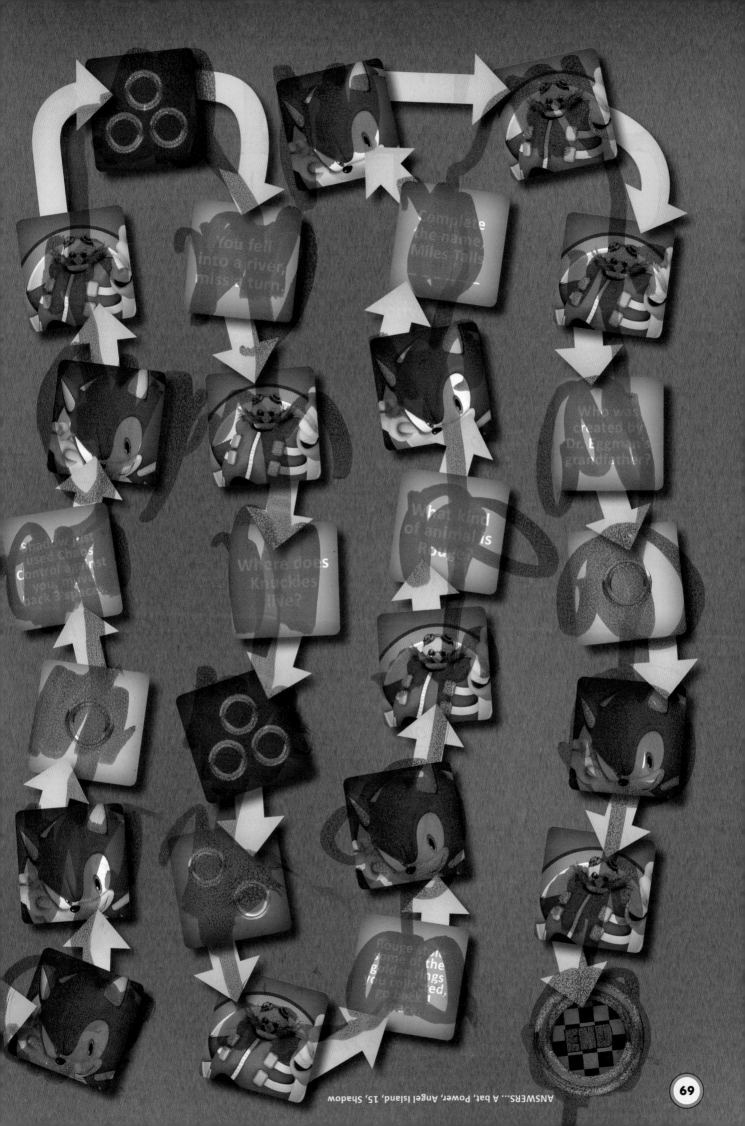

You fell into a river, miss a turn!

Complete the name: Miles Tails ___

Who was created by Dr. Eggman's grandfather?

Where does Knuckles live?

What kind of animal is Rouge?

Shadow just used Chaos Control against you, move back 3 spaces.

Rouge stole some of the gold rings you collected, go back...

CHARACTER CATCHPHRASE

Check out this list of catchphrases and sayings often used by Sonic and his friends, and Dr. Eggman and the bad guys. Read them carefully and think who is most likely to have said what. Then, simply draw a line to match the character to their catchphrase. Good luck!

"YOU NEVER CEASE TO SURPRISE ME, BLUE HEDGEHOG."

"I HATE THAT HEDGEHOG! HE RUINS MY SCHEMES!"

"I'M NOT SCARED. I'M NOT SCARED... I CAN DO THIS!"

"AS FAR BACK AS I CAN REMEMBER, I'VE BEEN LIVING ON THIS DARK ISLAND."

"I'M GOING TO HUNT FOR SOMEONE ELSE'S TREASURE!"

"HOLD ON, FROGGY! I'M COMING!"

"I FEEL THE NEED...THE NEED TO SPEED!"

"SONIC, GIVE UP AND BE MY BOYFRIEND. THIS TIME, YOU'RE MINE."

KNUCKLES' PICTURE PUZZLE

Using the type of skill which allows him to burrow like a mole, Knuckles has covered these pictures of our heroes, Sonic, Tails and Amy, in soil. In fact, all three of them are pretty much covered in muck! Looking carefully at what's left in each picture, can you identify which one's Sonic, which one's Tails and which one's Amy?

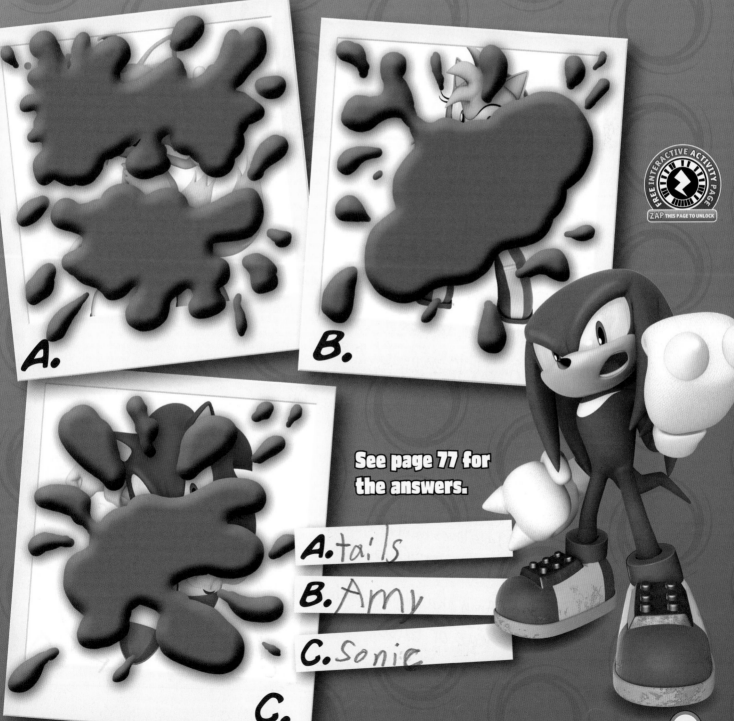

A.

B.

FREE INTERACTIVE ACTIVITY PAGE

ZAP THIS PAGE TO UNLOCK

See page 77 for the answers.

A. tails

B. Amy

C. Sonic

C.

THE BIG SONIC QUIZ PART THREE

It's time for the third and final round of The Big Sonic Quiz and the questions are getting even more difficult to answer. The next two pages feature 20 more tough questions about Sonic the Hedgehog. This time Shadow has joined Dr. Eggman and added plenty of misleading trick questions, so take your time and think each one through carefully...

1. Dr. Eggman is also known as Dr. Robotnik...
   True of False?

2. Knuckles favourite fruit is apples...
   True or False?

3. Amy is 10-years-old...
   True or False?

4. Shadow harnesses the power of seven Chaos Emeralds to become super Shadow...
   True or False?

5. Tails loves mint flavoured candy...
   True of False?

6. Amy and Big are both 18-years-old...
   True or False?

7. Sonic was born on Christmas Day...
   True or False?

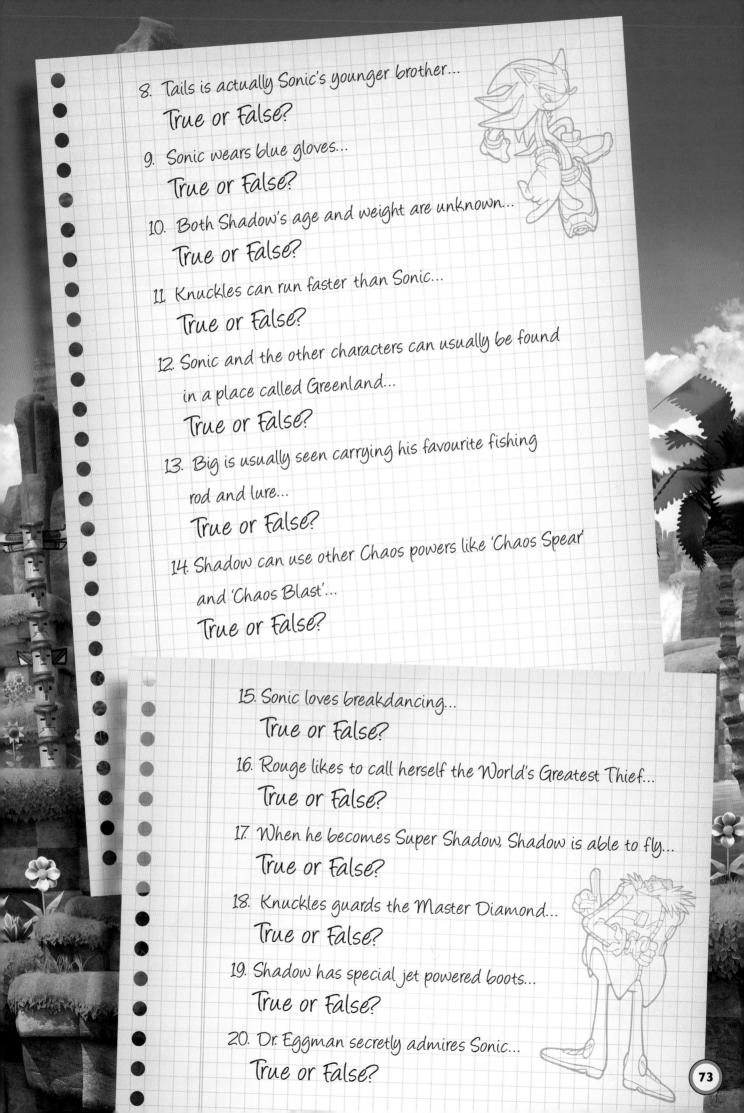

8. Tails is actually Sonic's younger brother...
   True or False?

9. Sonic wears blue gloves...
   True or False?

10. Both Shadow's age and weight are unknown...
    True or False?

11. Knuckles can run faster than Sonic...
    True or False?

12. Sonic and the other characters can usually be found
    in a place called Greenland...
    True or False?

13. Big is usually seen carrying his favourite fishing
    rod and lure...
    True or False?

14. Shadow can use other Chaos powers like 'Chaos Spear'
    and 'Chaos Blast'...
    True or False?

15. Sonic loves breakdancing...
    True or False?

16. Rouge likes to call herself the World's Greatest Thief...
    True or False?

17. When he becomes Super Shadow, Shadow is able to fly...
    True or False?

18. Knuckles guards the Master Diamond...
    True or False?

19. Shadow has special jet powered boots...
    True or False?

20. Dr. Eggman secretly admires Sonic...
    True or False?

DOUBLE DR. EGGMAN

The mischievous Dr. Eggman has been up to his usual tricks and invented another awesome machine. This one has a special laser ray that has made him invisible!

FREE INTERACTIVE ACTIVITY PAGE
ZAP THIS PAGE TO UNLOCK

The grid on page 74 shows what Dr. Eggman looked like before he used his machine to vanish into thin air. But how can Sonic defeat Eggman if he can't even see him? The only way to make the clever scientist reappear is to draw an exact replica of Dr. Eggman in the empty grid. Copy the detail, square by square in the grid below and help Sonic by bringing the Doctor back into view…

SONIC™
THE HEDGEHOG

FREE INTERACTIVE ACTIVITY PAGE
ZAP THIS PAGE TO UNLOCK

ANSWERS

Page 11

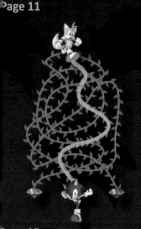

Page 15
EGGMAN'S IQ MATHS TEST
1. 25 x 4 = 100 + 50 = 150 + 50
= 200 + 100 = 300
2. 500 – 300 = 200 + 10 = 210 +
50 = 260 + 50 = 300 – 10 = 300
3. 3 x 10 = 30 + 100 = 130 + 20
= 150 x 2 = 300
4. 10 x 10 = 100 + 100 = 200 +
200 = 400 – 100 = 300
5. 100 + 50 = 150 – 100 = 50 +
200 = 250 + 20 = 270 + 10 = 280
+ 20 = 300

Page 16

Page 18

Page 20

Quick-Fire Quiz
(Shadow, Angel,
Black, Tails,
Rouge)

Final Answer:
Sonic the Hedgehog

Page 31

Page 32

Page 33
1. Dr. Eggman
2. Tails
3. Shadow
4. Knuckles
5. Rouge
   the Bat
6. Big the Cat
7. Sonic
8. Amy Rose

Page 34
THE BIG SONIC QUIZ
– PART ONE
1. True	8. True	15. True
2. False	9. False	16. True
3. False	10. False	17. True
4. True	11. True	18. True
5. True	12. True	19. False
6. False	13. False	20. False
7. True	14. True	

Page 36

Page 37
Shadow, Tails and Knuckles

Pages 38 and 39

Page 42
1. Tails
2. Amy
3. Knuckles
4. Shadow
5. Rouge
6. Big
7. Sonic
8. Dr. Eggman

Page 43
1. Knuckles
2. Shadow
3. Dr. Eggman

Page 44

Page 45
1. SONIC
2. ROUGE
3. TAILS
4. SHADOW
5. BIG
6. AMY
7. KNUCKLES

Page 46
Sonic
A loyal hedgehog who keeps his promises and never lets anybody down

Dr. Eggman
A mad scientist and an evil genius

Shadow
This character has a special power called 'Chaos Control'

Knuckles
This character can burrow like a mole

Tails
This foxcub is Sonic's most trusted companion

Rouge
A bat that loves hunting for jewels

Amy
This hedgehog wears pink and uses a Piko Piko hammer

Big
His best friend is called Froggy

Page 58

Page 59
1. Sonic
2. Tails
3. Shadow
4. Rouge
5. Big
6. Knuckles
7. Dr. Eggman
8. Amy

Page 60
THE BIG SONIC QUIZ
– PART TWO
1. True	8. True	15. False
2. False	9. True	16. False
3. True	10. False	17. True
4. False	11. False	18. True
5. False	12. True	19. False
6. False	13. False	20. True
7. True	14. True	

Page 62

Page 63

Pages 66 and 67

1. Shadow
2. Dr. Eggman
3. Sonic
4. Knuckles
5. Amy
6. Tails
7. Big
8. Rouge

Page 70
Dr. Eggman: "I hate that hedgehog! He ruins my schemes!"

Big the Cat: "Hold on, Froggy! I'm coming!"

Knuckles: "As far back as I can remember, I've been living on this dark island."

Tails: I'm not scared. I'm not scared...I can do this!"

Sonic: "I feel the need... the need to speed!" "

Shadow: "You never cease to surprise me, blue hedgehog."

Rouge the Bat: "I'm going to hunt for someone else's treasure!"

Amy Rose: "Sonic, give up and be my boyfriend. This time, you're mine."

Page 71
1. Sonic
2. Amy
3. Tails

Page 72
THE BIG SONIC QUIZ
– PART THREE
1. True	8. False	15. True
2. False	9. False	16. True
3. False	10. True	17. True
4. True	11. False	18. False
5. True	12. False	19. True
6. False	13. True	20. True
7. False	14. True	

Sonic the Hedgehog Annual 2014

Visit **Pedigreebooks.com** to find out
more on this year's **Sonic the Hedgehog Annual**,
scan with your mobile device to learn more.

Visit www.pedigreebooks.com

Pedigree Books, Beech Hill House, Walnut Gardens, Exeter EX4 4DH